SURREY
NARROW GAUGE
including South London

Vic Mitchell and Keith Smith

Middleton Press

Cover pictures:

Upper - The Standard Brick & Sand Company operated two substantial 0-6-0WTs near Redhill for many years. Seen in 1936 is Hudswell Clarke no. 1461 of 1929. (J.K.Williams coll.)

Lower - Preservation of industrial locomotives took place at Brockham Museum from the mid-1960s. Two diesels and some stock were recorded before the collection was moved to Amberley for enjoyment by all. (P.Nicholson)

Back - Authors Keith Smith (left) and Vic Mitchell squat beside no. 2 Northern Chief *at Hythe on 16th May 1999, prior to its departure with the 1.00pm book launch train for their* Romneyrail *album. (P.G.Barnes)*

Published January 2003

ISBN 1 901706 87 7

© *Middleton Press, 2003*

Design   Deborah Esher
             David Pede
Typesetting Barbara Mitchell

Published by
             Middleton Press
             Easebourne Lane
             Midhurst, West Sussex
             GU29 9AZ
Tel: 01730 813169
Fax: 01730 812601

Printed & bound by Biddles Ltd,
             Guildford and Kings Lynn

CONTENTS

SURREY

SOUTH LONDON

INTRODUCTION

The diverse uses of narrow gauge railways in Surrey resulted from its varied geology. The Chalk stretches from the Hogs Back near Farnham eastwards across the county to form the North Downs. These dip gently northwards towards the River Thames, in the valley of which gravel was extensively worked. South of the Downs, parallel outcrops of Sand were of economic importance, while the Chalk itself gave rise to limeworks. The Clay of The Weald of the south of Surrey supported a number of brickworks.

One of the earliest of the narrow gauge lines of Surrey and South London was the Surrey Iron Railway, its 4ft 2ins track running from Croydon, mainly through the Wandle Valley, to the Thames at Wandsworth. It was in use from 1803 to 1846 and linked with the Croydon, Merstham & Godstone Railway, which opened in 1805. However, it never reached Godstone, but the gauge has recently been confirmed by archaeologists.

There were other lines with little or no photographic record. These include those at Jesse Clack & Son's Beddington Brickworks and the nearby watercress beds. Many military lines tended to be elusive, such as those in the 22 miles of Chislehurst Caves (once in Surrey), when they were used for ammunition storage during World War I. There was also an extensive two-foot gauge system at the Royal Army Service Corp at Kidbrooke. It was also used by the Air Ministry and 12 different locomotives were recorded there.

The once extensive 2ft 7½ins gauge network at the gunpowder works at Chilworth is shown on a map in our *Guildford to Redhill* album, but no photographs are available.

Miniature railways are not included in this volume, but there are a number of references to photographs in the Middleton Press album *Industrial Railways of the South East* using the initials IRSE. The maps herein are to the scale of 25ins to 1 mile, unless otherwise indicated.

We are very grateful for the assistance received from those listed in the captions, and also L.Botting, R.M.Casserley, R.Howes, P.Sowan and C.Waters. As ever, our thanks go to Norman Langridge, David and Susan Salter and especially Janet Smith and Barbara Mitchell.

We hope that you will enjoy our selection.

Vic Mitchell and Keith Smith
January 2003

I.Location of narrow gauge lines featured in this book, in relation to some of the main railway routes. (D.H.Smith)

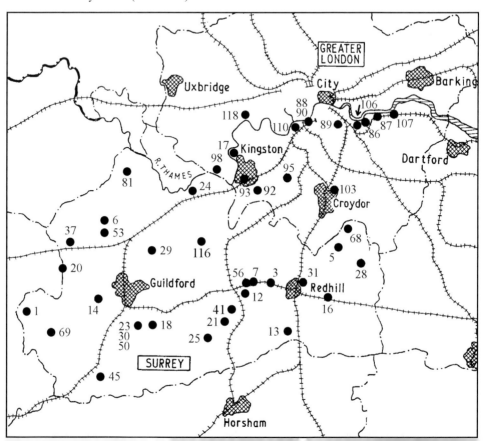

1. Industry
BALLAST PRODUCERS LTD.

1.   The Gravel pits were about one mile south-west of Farnham town centre and the locomotive on the left is near the entrance to the present carriage shed. On the right is one of the 20hp petrol engined Simplex locomotives built by Motor Rail for use in World War I. Three were used here, the last in 1952. (M.Hayter coll.)

2.   A different angle includes the grading plant where sand was separated from stone. There were few examples of parallel road and rail loading facilities. The Super Sentinel steam wagon was built in Shrewsbury and was first registered in 1924. (Farnham Herald/M.Hayter coll.)

Sports Ground

F.B

M.P.

II. The pit was operated by Thomas Patterson & Sons Ltd in its early years and is seen on the 1934 edition. The pit on the left became the site of the Southern Railway's rubbish tip. The west end of it was used for carriage sidings and a shed for electric trains in 1937.

Wey

Pit

S.R.

FARNHAM & ALTON LINE

S.P.

WEYDON LANE

TRAMWAY

TRAMWAY

Sand Pit

Weydon Hill Nursery

III. One mile east of Farnham station, there were other Wey Valley gravel pits. Here again there was a transfer facility adjacent to the SR. On the right is the original single track direct route to Ash via Tongham, which was closed to passengers in 1937.

ROAD

Gravel Pit

S.P.

Farnham Junction

S.B.

G.P.

251

S.P.

249

E.P.

245

243

M.S

L

Farnham 1
Guildford 9

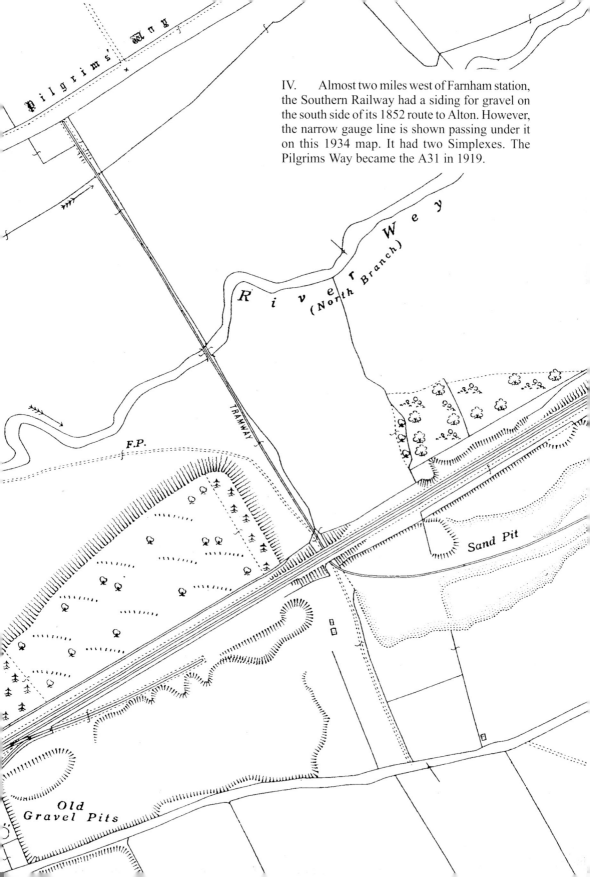

Pilgrims' Way

IV.   Almost two miles west of Farnham station, the Southern Railway had a siding for gravel on the south side of its 1852 route to Alton. However, the narrow gauge line is shown passing under it on this 1934 map. It had two Simplexes. The Pilgrims Way became the A31 in 1919.

River Wey (North Branch)

TRAMWAY

F.P.

Sand Pit

Old Gravel Pits

BUCKLAND SAND & SILICA CO. LTD.

3.   The pits were in the Upper Greensand, a strata found below the Chalk in both Surrey and Sussex. Two men are at work with shovels on the face; both seem precarious. (J.K.Williams coll.)

4.   A closer view of the locomotive in about 1935 shows it to be a Hudswell Clarke well tank. It had been supplied to the Air Ministry for use at its depot at Kidbrooke. Four new Simplexes were bought subsequently. (J.K.Williams coll.)

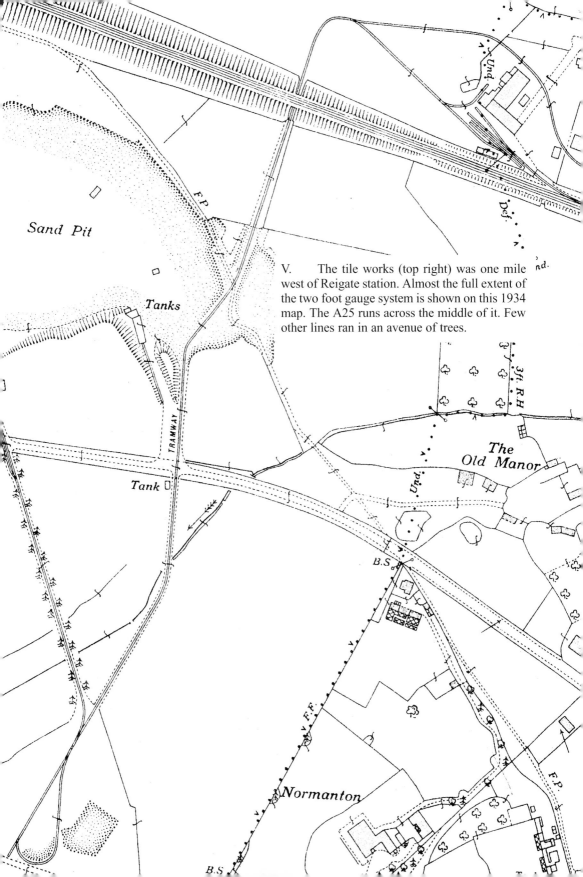

V. The tile works (top right) was one mile west of Reigate station. Almost the full extent of the two foot gauge system is shown on this 1934 map. The A25 runs across the middle of it. Few other lines ran in an avenue of trees.

5.   Beyond the jib of the Ruston Bucyrus shovel is part of the two-foot gauge line used for creating a new route for the A22, east of the town. It was completed in 1939 and included the first roundabout to have a pedestrian subway. (C.Shepheard coll.)

DAYDAWN NURSERIES LTD.

6.   This two-foot gauge line was created on a site near Bisley. This view was recorded on 28th December 1971. The locomotive was a Hibberd diesel of 20hp, built in 1943 as no. 2834. It was used by Hall & Co. Ltd. at Waltham Cross until about 1965. The railway was owned by J.E.Barton until the end of 1971 and the locomotive was sold to M.E.Engineering in May 1972. A further sale in April 1975 found the machine in Kent in the care of Best Bros, operators of the Bredgar & Wormshill Railway. It subsequently went to the Leighton Buzzard Light Railway. (P.Nicholson)

DORKING GREYSTONE
LIME CO. LTD.

VI. The quarry was about halfway between Dorking and Reigate, north of the village of Betchworth, and was worked until the early 1970s. The track complex is shown on the 1934 6ins to 1 mile map, along with that at the adjacent Brockham Lime Works, which closed in 1936. The lines there were never locomotive worked.

7.	Most of the tracks were laid to the unusual gauge of 3ft 2¼ins and are seen with one of the two Fletcher Jennings 0-4-0Ts purchased in 1880. A hand-worked winch stands at the top of the incline, but subsequently it was replaced by a pulley around which a rope passed to the locomotive on the lower level. (J.K.Williams coll.)

9.	This view was taken from the footbridge over the line, the path being usually regarded as the Pilgrims Way. In the distance is Betchworth station and its adjacent inn, while on the right is the eastern battery of kilns. The lime was withdrawn at a lower level. (J.A.Peden/A.Neale coll.)

8.	A panorama from around 1900 reflects the demand for lime in this period. The chalk dust encrusted wagons near the Fletcher Jennings loco are barely visible in this total chalk environment. Two lines were built later: one of two-foot gauge and the other of 1ft 7ins. (A Neale coll.)

Other views can be found in pictures 86 to 93 in our *Guildford to Redhill* album, also IRSE 63 to 70.

10. This is Fletcher Jennings no. 1732 prior to its acquisition of a new boiler in about 1898. Its owners later gave it the number 5 and the name *William Finlay*, after the firm's founder. The 3ft 2¼ins lines ceased to be used in 1954. Also from the same builder was *Dolgoch* on the Talyllyn Railway. It shares many of the same features, but has a longer wheelbase. (J.K.Williams coll.)

11. The companion locomotive was no. 4 *Townsend Hook* and it was recorded on 10th April 1960 being removed for preservation by the Narrow Gauge Railway Society. It has been at the Amberley Working Museum in recent years. (J.K.Williams coll.)

12.   Vast tonnages of chalk had to be moved to create a new route for the A29 in 1926. The Surrey County Council employed its own steam shovel to load the two-foot gauge trains.
(C.Shepheard coll.)

GATWICK BRICK CO. LTD.

13.   Hookwood Brickworks was situated about 1½ miles west of Horley station and it had about 100yds of track. It used four different Motor Rail products; this is no. 4802/34. It was photographed on 30th March 1968 and was subsequently scrapped. (P.Nicholson)

GUILDFORD BYPASS

14.   The construction of this road necessitated heavy civil engineering, as it cut through the Chalk mass of the Hogs Back. Surrey County Council Highways Department employed Hudswell Clarke 0-6-0WT no. 1645/30 and it appears in IRSE in picture no. 51. It was sold to the Charlton Sand & Ballast Co. Ltd at Littleton in 1935. Major earthworks were necessary at the southern end of the bypass where a bridge was required over the River Wey. (C.Shepheard coll.)

15.   The SCC Ruston-Bucyrus steam shovel is loading a train on the alignment of the new A3, where it passes under the A31. The work was undertaken in 1931 using a fund set up by Mayor William Harvey to relieve unemployment. (C.Shepheard coll.)

HAM RIVER GRIT CO. LTD.
Bletchingley Pits

16.　　The site was almost four miles east of Redhill station and was concerned with sand extraction. It was operated by Town Farm Sand Pits Ltd previously and it had a two-foot gauge line. Motor Rail no. 7188 was a regular worker. Seen on 12th April 1963, near the tip, is Motor Rail no. 7215 running as L08. The Simplex product lasted much longer than its wartime designers anticipated. Five similar machines are known to have worked here, plus two 0-4-0STs. (C.G.Down)

HAM RIVER GRIT CO. LTD
Ham Pits

17.   Seen on this two-foot gauge system on 23rd June 1932 is Bagnall 0-4-0ST no. 2079/18. Four similar Kerr Stuart locos were used here at different times, also 15 different internal combustion machines. The pits were near the Thames, between Kingston and Richmond. Within 20 years, the firm had five other pits. (J.K.Williams coll.)

A. HONE & SONS LTD.

18.   Ewhurst Brickworks was about three miles east of Cranleigh, near Somerbury Wood, and it used a two-foot gauge line for clay transport. Photographed on 3rd April 1971 was battery-electric locomotive no. 6693 from Wingrove & Rogers. (P.Nicholson)

19.   Seen on the same day in the pit was the firm's Ruston & Hornsby diesel. Tipping sticky clay in Winter could be unsuccessful, as the wagon would sometimes follow the load. (P.Nicholson)

INNS & CO. LTD.

FARNBOROUGH

20.   Although Farnborough is in Hampshire, half of the gravel pits were in Surrey, being east of the Blackwater River. They were located immediately south of North Camp station. The photo of Motor Rail no. 7467 was taken in June 1964; the line was short lived and had gone by 1967. (C.G.Down)

LONDON BRICK COMPANY

21.   Clock House Works was built 1½ miles south-east of Ockley station and the same distance south of Capel village. On the first floor of the brick kiln was a 2ft 11ins line, with a third rail for electric current supply. There was also a 3ft 11ins track. The photo is from March 1968. (P.Nicholson)

22.   There was still evidence of the former two-foot gauge system outside its workshop in 2002. The line had been worked by four different four-wheeled diesels. There is a former tipper body below the notice board. (P.G.Barnes)

MANFIELD BRICKWORKS

23.   Two different locos had worked on the clay pit line, which was one mile east of Cranleigh. A Hibberd was recorded in March 1963, the haulage having been cable since 1955. (C.G.Down)

NORTH SURREY WATER

24.　　The photograph was taken near Walton-on-Thames on 20th March 2001. The 3ft 6ins gauge Keef 55 of 1998, in white livery, is seen stabled beside the semi-treated water reservoirs in the middle of four wagons. Each wagon contains powered rollers used for laying and collecting floating covers to and from the reservoirs. The loco only sees occasional use on the four hundred yards of straight track and there is not a resident driver. Movements are therefore carried out by Alan Keef Ltd. staff when required. (E.Knotwell)

OCKLEY (SURREY) BRICK, TILE AND POTTERY COMPANY

25.　　Smokejacks Brickworks was situated near a farm of that name, two miles south-west of Ockley. Wingrove & Rogers battery electric locomotive no. 6693 was recorded on 20th September 1966. (C.G.Down)

26.   A closer view in March 1965 includes the locomotive shed, which housed a fleet of two-foot gauge Orenstein & Koppel diesels. Their fuel source is on the right. (C.G.Down)

27.   The firm also had a Ruston & Hornsby on hire from ME Engineering in March 1968. Its works number was 223702. (P.Nicholson)

OXTED GREYSTONE LIME COMPANY

28.   The works was located one mile on the London side of Oxted station and main line sidings were in place until 1969, although long disused. Seen on the 2ft gauge line in October 1967 is Orenstein & Koppel no. 7600. A smoking limekiln and the Weald are on the left. (P.Nicholson)

VII.   The 1912 map has the standard gauge sidings at the bottom. Their connection to the LBSCR can be seen in picture 64 in our *Croydon to East Grinstead* album. Also see IRSE 62.

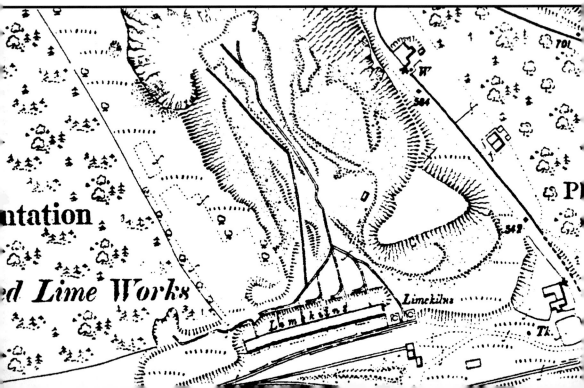

REDLAND PIPES LTD

29.   The pipe works was near Ripley and the two-foot gauge circular line was used to reach the stacking ground. Orenstein & Koppel no. 6193 was photographed on 7th April 1968; it eventually became an exhibit at the Amberley Working Museum. (P.Nicholson)

SMITHBROOK BRICKWORKS (1936) LTD.

30.   The short line near Cranleigh was usually worked by hand and thus this Lister diesel spent most of its time in the shed. It was recorded in January 1965, its gauge being 2ft. (C.G.Down)

31.   An extensive two foot gauge system was in use at Holmethorpe, one mile north of Redhill. Hudswell Clarke no. 1314 was supplied to the RAF in 1918 and had several owners before coming here in about 1935. (J.K.Williams coll.)

32.   From the same builder was no. 1461, a 1929 model. It arrived here in 1936, after working for at least two other firms. It also appears on the cover of this book. (J.K.Williams coll.)

33.   Part of the massive pit is evident as track lifting was recorded on 31st March 1963. No. 1 was a Ruston & Hornsby diesel. (C.G.Down)

3 ft. R.H.

3 ft. F F

OLD S.E. & C.R. MAIN LINE

Mission Hall

Battlebridge
Brick & Tile Works

R O A D

Smithy

S.P

TRAMWAY

W

W

Siding Brick

TRAMWAY

Chy
Kilns

F R E N C H ' S

M.P

S.P

Holmethorpe

E   R O A D

RDON ROAD

S.B.

F.B.

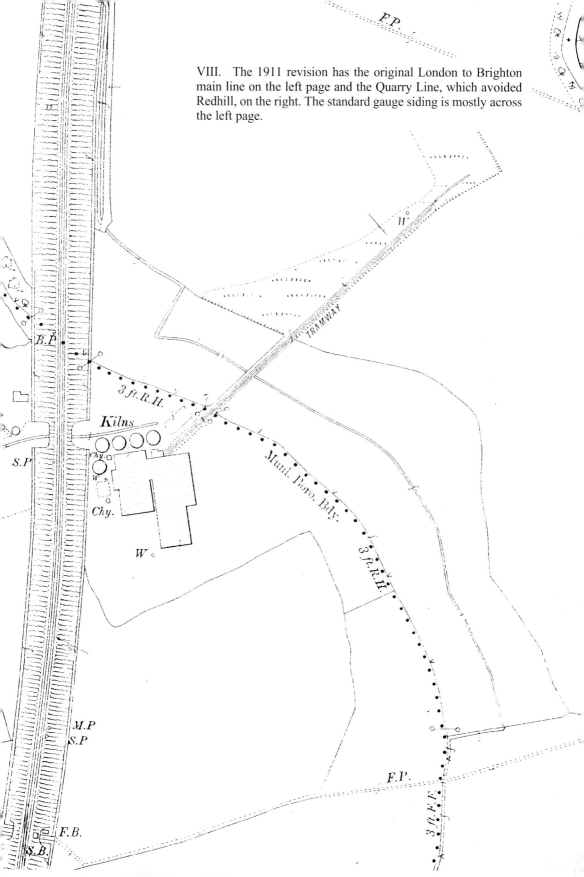

VIII. The 1911 revision has the original London to Brighton main line on the left page and the Quarry Line, which avoided Redhill, on the right. The standard gauge siding is mostly across the left page.

34.   On the same day, two other Rustons were at work near the stock pile. Note that the train includes a fuel tank wagon. There had been 17 diesels in use on the system over the years. (C.G.Down)

35.   Seldom photographed was O&K no. 4371, which pulled the traversers that gave access to the brick curing autoclaves. A brick stack awaits on the right. See also IRSE 9 to 12. (C.G.Down)

36.   The end is nigh as three Rustons await their fate on 4th July 1965. British Industrial Sand supplied the glass making industry via its standard gauge siding, which is illustrated in pictures 55-57 in *East Croydon to Three Bridges*. (A.Neale)

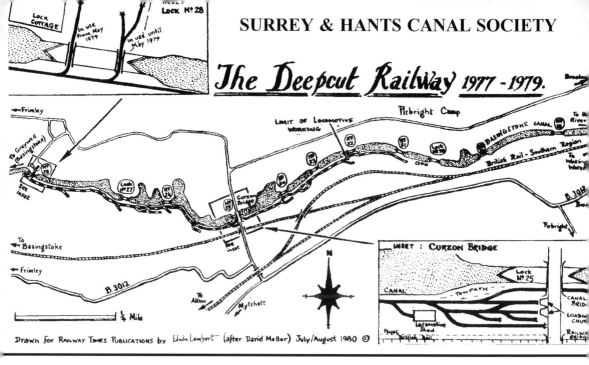

Drawn for Railway Times Publications by Edwin Lambert (after David Mellor) July/August 1980 ©

IX.   The society was formed in 1966 to campaign for the restoration of the Basingstoke Canal and, after ten years, its control passed to the two county councils concerned. A railway group was established by volunteers in 1975 to facilitate work remote from roads and it was active in Surrey in 1977-79. (D.Mellor)

37.   Hunslet diesel no. 1944 of 1939 was acquired from ME Engineering and is seen on a temporary bridge over lock no. 28, together with one of two man riding cars constructed by the group. Two bogie wagons were built for scaffold conveyance. The locomotive is now based on the Old Kiln Light Railway.   (P.Nicholson)

38. The same two items are seen during a propelling operation on the well-sleepered track. Equipment came from a variety of sources, including Chichester Sewage Works. (P.Nicholson)

39. Two views from 2nd July 1978 feature the same locomotive. Here it is passing under Curzon Bridge, between lock no. 25 and the loading shute, near Pirbright. (P.Nicholson)

40.   Sand, cement, bricks (left) and other materials were conveyed for lock restoration. The gap will receive a gate recess; the groove is for stop boards, used when the canal needs to be shut off. (P.Nicholson)

SUSSEX AND DORKING UNITED BRICK CO. LTD.
North Holmwood

41.　　This brickworks was about two miles south of Dorking and it had a two foot gauge system with an unusual driverless battery electric locomotive (Wingrove & Rogers no. 4998). After loading the train, the operator simply set it away. The loco is now at the Amberley Working Museum. (P.Nicholson)

42.　　A ramp between the rails (left) could stop the train if the points (out of view, to the right) were wrongly set. The rod in the foreground linked the two. The incline in the background was rope worked. (P.Nicholson)

43.   A second fixed ramp beyond the points would stop the locomotive automatically. There was also a conventional locomotive (W&R no. 4634/51), which could be driven if the other failed. (P.Nicholson)

44.   There was a second incline, which outlasted the other. Three four-wheeled diesels were known to have been used. The works closed in 1981. See also IRSE 4-7. (C.M.Jackson)

Nutbourne Brickworks

45.   This site was 1¼ miles east of Witley station, near the village of Hambledon and was photographed in April 1980. A Lister-powered Motor Rail diesel stands near an electrically driven excavator of some antiquity. (C.M.Jackson)

46.   Another Motor Rail diesel was recorded near its fuel source. The system was a late closure. Both works became part of Redland Bricks. (C.M.Jackson)

47.   Three views from 4th May 1968 show earlier Motor Rails that worked on the premises. This is no. 5808. (P.Nicholson)

48.   No. 7173 was fitted with some notable derailing bars. Temporary track on soft clay was prone to move readily, particularly in Winter. (P.Nicholson)

49.   No. 8678 did have some weather protection for the driver, but it was of limited value with a cross wind. Most of the side tippers were unsprung and built by Hudsons. (P.Nicholson)

SWALLOW'S TILES (CRANLEIGH) LTD.

50. Our photographic survey was made on 20th September 1966. There was typical clay pit track chaos with fragments of two foot gauge track scattered around, some of it manufactured Jubilee panels. (C.G.Down)

51. Most skip movement was by hand, the slatted duckboards being provided for the trammer to obtain a good foothold above the slippery clay. A Ruston & Hornsby diesel was obtained from the nearby Manfield Brickworks in about 1953, but it was more trouble than it was worth. (C.G.Down)

52. The sheeted wagon is about to be hauled up the incline by cable to the works, while empties wait to be pushed back to the pit. (C.G.Down)

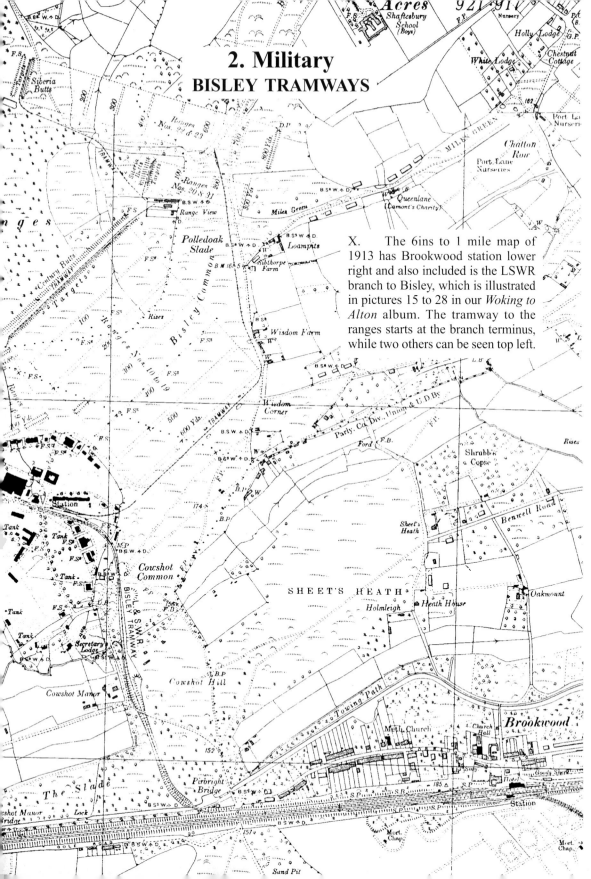

2. Military
BISLEY TRAMWAYS

X. The 6ins to 1 mile map of 1913 has Brookwood station lower right and also included is the LSWR branch to Bisley, which is illustrated in pictures 15 to 28 in our *Woking to Alton* album. The tramway to the ranges starts at the branch terminus, while two others can be seen top left.

53. The National Rifle Association was formed in 1859 and used Wimbledon Common for its annual meetings. Temporary two foot gauge track was used there but the lease expired in 1888 and the NRA soon moved to Bisley. However, it was not until 1898 that they unpacked their track, stock and their 1877 Merryweather steam tram named *Wharncliffe* after their chairman. (J.K.Williams coll.)

54. The separate lines to the Siberia and Century Butts were laid in about 1900. The latter is seen in two photographs from December 1971. A Lister diesel resided in the shed. (P.Nicholson)

55. The line served the targets which are seen in the background. The dates of the demise of the three routes cannot be traced. (P.Nicholson)

56.   A group of members of the Narrow Gauge Railway Society saved some stock of the Betchworth Quarry railways in the early 1960s and leased part of the adjacent Brockham Quarry for its storage, starting work on the site in January 1962. This view from March 1968 features a Planet petrol locomotive. (F.Hornby)

57.   The Brockham Museum Association was formed in 1966 and the Trust followed in 1972. More stock and rails continued to arrive from diverse sources. The coach was from RAF Fauld, Staffordshire, the front locomotive is a Ransomes & Rapier and the rear one is a Ruston & Hornsby. Two were needed because of the steep gradient. This is May 1970. (P.Nicholson)

58.   A brick archway and adjacent embankment had to be removed to create a running line. *The Major* was an Orenstein & Koppel diesel, built in 1937, and is seen on 24th April 1971. (P.Nicholson)

59.   The limeworks had closed in 1936 and only the kilns, a cottage and the stables remained. The latter became the museum's workshop and these locomotive sheds had to be built. Centre stage is *The Major*; each side of it are Ruston & Hornsbys, newly arrived from Eastbury Pumping Station, Oxhey, Herts. Their works numbers are shown in chalk on 10th February 1968. (P.Nicholson)

60.   The variety of locomotives steadily increased. No. 22 is a Ruston & Hornsby (works no. 226302) of 1944 and on the left is a Lister (works no. 9256) of 1937. (P.Nicholson)

61.   As on the Festiniog Railway's Deviation Project, embankments were created using one Hudson tipper mounted transversely on the frame of another. The assembly is also seen in picture 58. The date is 29th March 1970. (P.Nicholson)

62.   Recorded in 1972 is Ruston & Hornsby diesel no. 2 (no. 166024 of 1933). The RAF personnel coach is in the background. Public access to the site presented many problems, as did the neighbours. (D.Trevor Rowe)

63.   Another 1972 photograph and this features two Fowler diesels rescued from the cement works at Cliffe-at-Hoo, in Kent. On the left is de Winton 0-4-0VB *Llanfair*, which was later moved to the Oakeley Quarry at Blaenau Ffestiniog. (C.M.Jackson)

64. By April 1976, the collection had grown greatly, but so had the difficulties mentioned earlier. The kilns are obvious; the quarry face is less so. (F.Hornby)

65. Finally we have three photographs from 17th August 1980. Featured here is 0-4-0ST *Peter* awaiting some TLC. It was built by Bagnall in 1918. No. 5 was the Museum's only coach. (J.H.Meredith)

66.   Displayed on a plinth is a 2ft 11ins side discharge clay wagon from the London Brick Company's Arlesey Works. Behind is a 5ft 3ins converter bogie into which the hoist dropped a 2ft gauge locomotive to shunt the Guiness Works in Dublin. In the background is *Townsend Hook*. (J.H.Meredith)

67.   *Townsend Hook* was one of the treasures rescued from Betchworth, but being of 3ft 2¼ins gauge it was not operated. It was created in 1880 by Fletcher Jennings in Whitehaven. (J.H.Meredith)

XI.   This ambitious plan was drawn up, but the shaded area never materialised. Owing to the local difficulties, it was resolved to move most of the collection to the developing industrial museum at Amberley. This took place in 1981-83 and the resulting splendid combination is extensively illustrated in our companion album, *Sussex Narrow Gauge*. Amberley Working Museum received a Heritage Lottery Grant of £108,000 in June 2002 to increase the covered accommodation so that all the historic stock could be properly housed. (D.H.Smith)

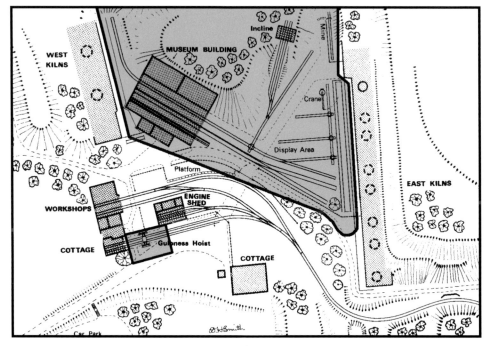

GARDNER'S PLEASURE RESORT, RIDDLESDOWN

68.   William George Gardner purchased the site in 1892 and opened the railway in the following year. He is thought to have built the locomotive, which is believed to have survived until about 1948. The line had closed by 1934, but its gauge is not known. (J.K.Williams coll.)

OLD KILN LIGHT RAILWAY, TILFORD

XII.   The line grew within the Rural Life Centre, near Tilford, from January 1982 onwards and is operated by a small group independent of the RLC. The diagram is not to scale, but shows the halt names as revised for the 2002 season. The railway runs on Sundays and Bank Holidays in the Summer and is about a third of a mile long. (R.Neal)

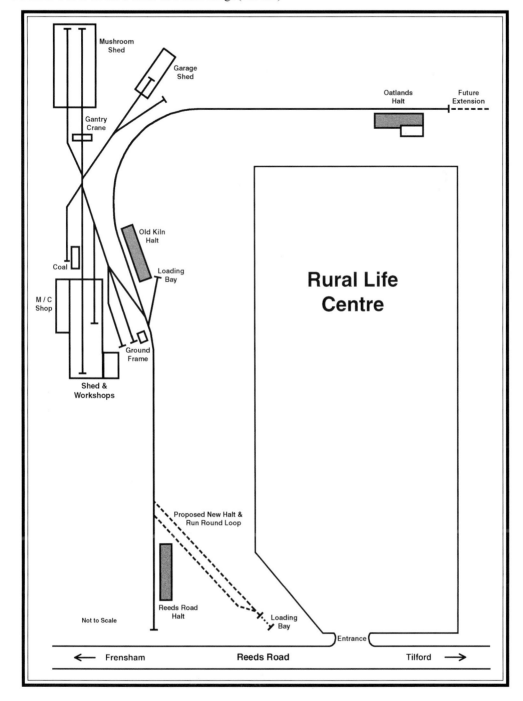

Mushroom Shed

Garage Shed

Oatlands Halt

Future Extension

Gantry Crane

Old Kiln Halt

Coal

Loading Bay

M / C Shop

Rural Life Centre

Ground Frame

Shed & Workshops

Proposed New Halt & Run Round Loop

Reeds Road Halt

Not to Scale

Loading Bay

Entrance

← Frensham   Reeds Road   Tilford →

69.   Old Kiln Halt became Reeds Road Halt in 2002, being close to that highway, which runs along the southern boundary of the site. The 1922 Orenstein & Koppel 0-6-0WT *Elouise* was recorded on "Rustic Sunday", 29th July 2001. (P.G.Barnes)

70.   This and the following seven photos were taken at the works, the designation Old Kiln Halt being transferred to the platform there in 2002. *Jack* was visiting for the 1998 Gala Weekend, it having spent its working life at Glasgow Corporation Gasworks. (G.Neal/OKLR)

71.   *Elouise* stands behind *Sue* on 19th September 1999. This diminutive 0-2-2-0 is an occasional visitor here. (G.Neal/OKLR)

72.   A glimpse in the cab of *Sue* reveals part of the single expansion engine therein. It drives the rear axle by means of a chain.
(G.Neal/OKLR)

73.   In the absence of run-round loops, the loco propels the coaches in the southward direction. Two Baguley coaches are seen in July 2001 attached to *Elouise*, the engine being air braked. (P.G.Barnes)

74.   The railway's splendid replica Glyn Valley Tramway coach is seen in 1999. Behind it is a brake van from the Royal Naval Armament Depot at Dean Hill, near Romsey.
(R.Neal/OKLR)

75. The platform is in the foreground as Ruston & Hornsby no. 392117 *Norden* stands in front of the two covered coaches. It was built in 1956 for work on the quadrupling scheme at Hadley Wood and was later sold to Fayles Tramway - see *Branch Line to Swanage*. (R.Bentley)

76. Ruston & Hornsby No. 181820 *Red Dwarf* stands outside the engine shed in the Summer of 2001. It was originally used by Severn Trent Water Authority to maintain the banks of the River Severn in the Gloucester area. (R.Bentley)

77. The line has about ten industrial diesel engines. Motor Rail No. 5713 *Eagle* stands with one of the Baguley coaches. It was built to operate at the Staveley Coal & Iron Co. site in Chesterfield. Having worked at several pipe and brick works in the Chesterfield area, the loco was preserved and moved south, initially to Brockham Museum. (R.Bentley)

78. *Elouise* approaches the eastern terminus, Oatlands Halt, with a Santa Special in December 1999. The other steam locomotive on the site is the 1906 Hunslet 0-4-0ST *Pamela* and is ex-Penrhyn Quarry. (R.Bentley)

79. The tiny waiting room could accommodate about six (standing), provided that the coal fired stove was not too hot. The Oatlands sign came from a signal box, between Walton-on-Thames and Weybridge. (P.G.Barnes)

OATLANDS

OLD KILN LIGHT RAILWAY

DAILY MAIL

STEAM TRAIN RIDES

SURREY LIGHT RAILWAY

80.   *Peter Pan* was built by Kerr Stuart in 1922 and was recorded at Southwood Manor Farm, near Hersham, on 30th April 1978. This private railway was unusual in being fully track circuited for its colour light signals. *Peter Pan* has subsequently been a star of the show at the Leighton Buzzard Railway. (P.Nicholson)

THORPE PARK, CHERTSEY

TREASURE ISLAND RAILWAY

81.   Two photographs from 12th April 1984 show parts of this two-foot gauge entertainment line, a few days after it opened. Few railways bisect a pirate ship. (P.Nicholson)

82.   Both locomotives were built by Alan Keef Ltd and were works numbers 11 and 12, although TIR002 and TIR001 in traffic. The former became *Ivor* and was used for shunting, while the latter moved to the Lynbarn Railway in Devon and was named *Sir George*. Each of the two trains were composed of four coaches. (P.Nicholson)

83.   This line had three Severn Lamb 4-4-0 locomotives, two built in 1989 and one in 1994. They each had a diesel engine in the tender. (A.James)

WEY VALLEY LIGHT RAILWAY

84.   This was created by members of the Narrow Gauge Railway Society at the Old Pumping Station, Guildford Road, Farnham. Some skip frames were adapted for passenger carriage by the Venture Scouts and were taken to the Farnham Town Show from 1971 onwards, together with a small petrol locomotive. (P.Nicholson)

85.   Almost 1000 passengers were carried in the three days of the first show visited, but their Ruston & Hornsby and Hibberd diesels were too heavy to transport easily, so their Petter petrol engine provided haulage. Most of the equipment formed the nucleus of the Old Kiln Light Railway in 1982. (P.Nicholson)

SOUTH LONDON

4. Industry

BRITISH ROPES, CHARLTON

86.   The firm had two Ruston & Hornsby diesels, nos. 193970 and 203010, the latter being seen off the rails on 3rd April 1965. Prior to these, two petrol-engined machines had been in use. The track was of two-foot gauge. (C.G.Down)

GASWORKS

London's major gasworks had relatively little use for main line railways, although the biggest works acquired connections eventually. Almost all coal came by sea, but some coke was later sent away by rail. Within the works it was a different matter, for most had internal railway networks of various gauges. Narrow-gauge "coaling tramways" became popular from about 1860 and were often on cast-iron viaducts. Typically, trollies holding 20cwt of coal were manually propelled; the same trollies could carry 11cwt of coke. Hydraulic lifts connected the high and low level tracks. The more modern works were less congested and had no need of narrow gauge, especially after coal and coke conveyors were developed.

In the 1890s small steam locomotives were widely adopted and several pioneer petrol and diesel engines later gave long service in South London gasworks. The narrow gauge latterly played a reduced role hauling ash and breeze, for example. This ended when coal carbonisation ceased at most works in the 1950s, although some systems closed earlier.

There was an elusive narrow gauge network at the Bankside Works, which did not appear on maps as it was entirely roofed over. The works closed in 1938 and the site was used for a power station, which is now the Tate Modern. It is between Southwark and Blackfriars Bridges.

East Greenwich

87.   South London's (and the South Metropoitan's) largest gas works was using almost half a million tons of coal per annum by 1913 and later double that. There was plenty of space and the 750mm (2ft 5½ins) network was small, mostly around the oxide purifiers. The locomotives were numbered with the much larger standard-gauge fleet; no. 14 was the tiny Avonside 143/01. Nos. 8, 11 and 18 were Bagnalls. This is no. 8 shortly before closure of the narrow gauge system in 1933, but the works lasted until 1976. The site was redeveloped at the end of the century for The Dome. (J.K.Williams coll.)

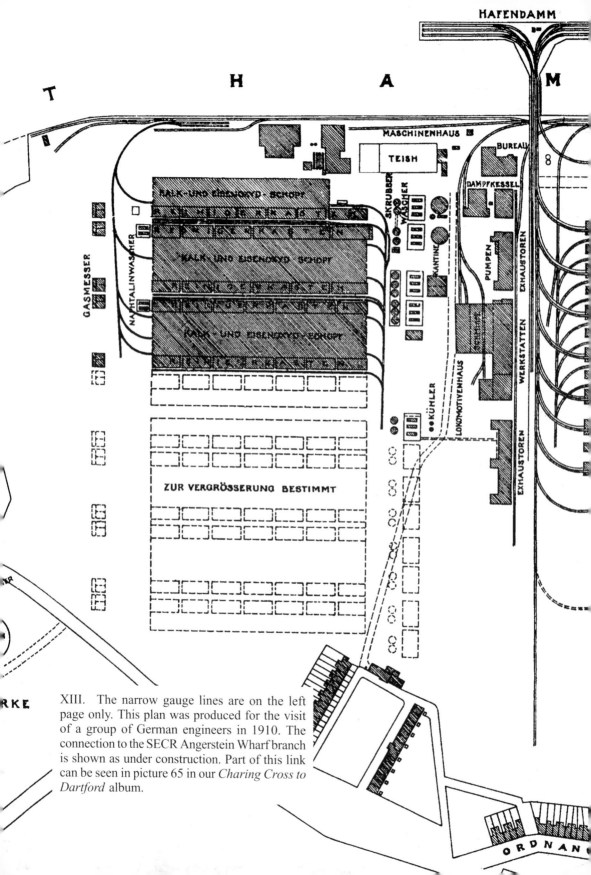

HAFENDAMM

T　　　H　　　A　　　M

MASCHINENHAUS

TEISH

BUREAU

DAMPFKESSEL

SKRUBBER

WÄSCHER

KANTINE

PUMPEN

EXHAUSTOREN

WERKSTÄTTEN

KALK- UND EISENOXYD- SCHOPF

KALK- UND EISENOXYD SCHOPF

KALK - UND EISENOXYD- SCHOPF

GASMESSER

NAPHTALINWÄSCHER

KÜHLER

LOKOMOTIVENHAUS

EXHAUSTOREN

ZUR VERGRÖSSERUNG BESTIMMT

RKE

ORDNAN

XIII. The narrow gauge lines are on the left page only. This plan was produced for the visit of a group of German engineers in 1910. The connection to the SECR Angerstein Wharf branch is shown as under construction. Part of this link can be seen in picture 65 in our *Charing Cross to Dartford* album.

D

E S

SÄUREANLAGE Nº1

SÄUREANLAGE Nº2

SÄUREANLAGE Nº3

SÄUREANLAGE Nº4

SÄURE - UND AMMONIAK - WERKE

H L E R
ENLAGER
ORTENHAUS Nº1
LENLAGER
ORTENHAUS Nº2
LENLAGER
ORTENHAUS Nº3
LENLAGER
ORTENHAUS Nº4
LENLAGER

LENLAGER
ORTENHAUS Nº5
LENLAGER

GRIESWASCHEREI
KOKSSIEBE
KOKSBRECHER
KOKSPLATE

ANSCHLUSSGELEISE ZUR S.E.&C EISENBAHN

VERGRÖSSERUNG BESTIMMT

HAUPTTOR ZU DEN WERKEN

S T R E E
E N F E L
R D STREET

GASBEHALTER
244.370 cbm.

Nine Elms

The works was built by the London Gas Light Co. and first made gas in 1863. It passed to the Gas, Light & Coke Co. in 1883, their only works south of the river. It had extensive coaling viaducts from at least 1879. The original lines took coal from the enclosed barge dock, but the viaduct was later extended across Nine Elms Lane to the ship dock. A double track inclined plane was rope worked at that point but the remaining half-mile or so of main line and branches was hand-worked.

The original system appears to have used the popular three-foot gauge, but later a third rail was added to several tracks and at least one two-foot gauge locomotive was introduced. This was *Iris*, an 0-4-0 Bagnall of the type which its makers called an "inverted saddle tank". The two foot system did not cross Nine Elms Lane and may therefore have been confined to coke and breeze in side-tipping wagons. However, it is more likely to have assisted the reclamation of coal from stock piles since coal arrived by sea at a fairly steady rate, whereas the demand for gas peaked in Winter.

The works was converted to conveyor belts in 1926-27 and although the viaducts remained for some time, the railways probably saw little if any use thereafter. The coal tonnage carbonised rose from about 121,000 tons in 1882 to 200,000 tons in 1910. When the conveyor belts took over, the tramways were importing about 280,000 tons per annum, some of which was hauled twice since it had to be reclaimed from stock.

88a.   The three-rail sections are blurred on the map, but this photograph shows clearly a length passing under three conveyors with the massive no. 3 gas holder in the background. (J.B.Horne coll.)

88b. This is a northward view of the 3ft gauge double track over Nine Elms Road, with the collier *SS Afterglow* being unloaded. The barge canal is to the right of it. (J.B.Horne coll.)

The Gas Engineer reproduced this engraving of *Iris* in 1898.

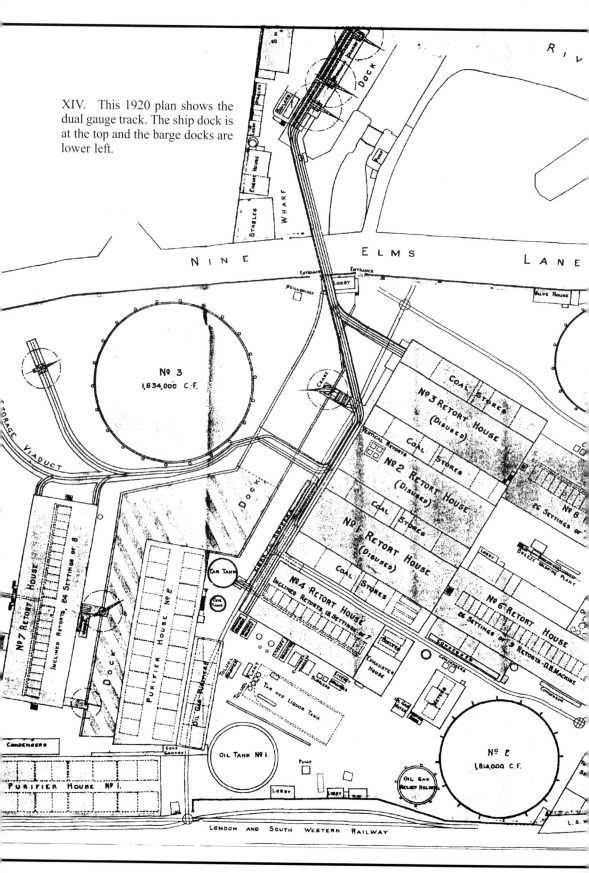

XIV. This 1920 plan shows the dual gauge track. The ship dock is at the top and the barge docks are lower left.

Old Kent Road

This was the headquarters of the South Metropolitan Gas Company and their original works, started in 1834. All other South Metropolitan works were on the river; this one took its coal via the Surrey Canal. The first locomotive was *Concord* (Bagnall no. 1421/92) and it is not certain that there were tracks here before that date. The gauge was 3ft.

The railway was extensive and handled both coal and coke; the second locomotive *Unity* (Bagnall no. 1534/98) was an identical 2-4-0T; they were reminiscent of those of the Rye & Camber and the Groudle Glen Railways. The names chosen at OKR reflected the Co-Partnership scheme which flourished in the pre-nationalisation gas industry and kept the South Metropolitan strike-free. The railway worked, on a reduced scale, until the works ceased production in 1953. OKR processed 216,000 tons of coal per annum in 1913 and remained fairly constant through the first half of the twentieth century.

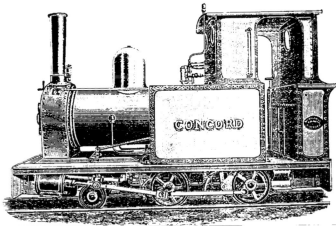

89. *Unity* was sold to Cashmore for scrapping in 1955 and was recorded in front of *Concord*, long before supersonic travellers came to use the name.
(J.K.Williams coll.)

Concord also appeared in *The Gas Engineer* in 1898, the reproduction showing clearly one of its cylinders which were only 7 x 11 ins.

XV.   The 1950 map shows the full extent of the system and has the Surrey Canal at the top. The street tramway is included in *Southwark and Deptford Tramways.* (Middleton Press)

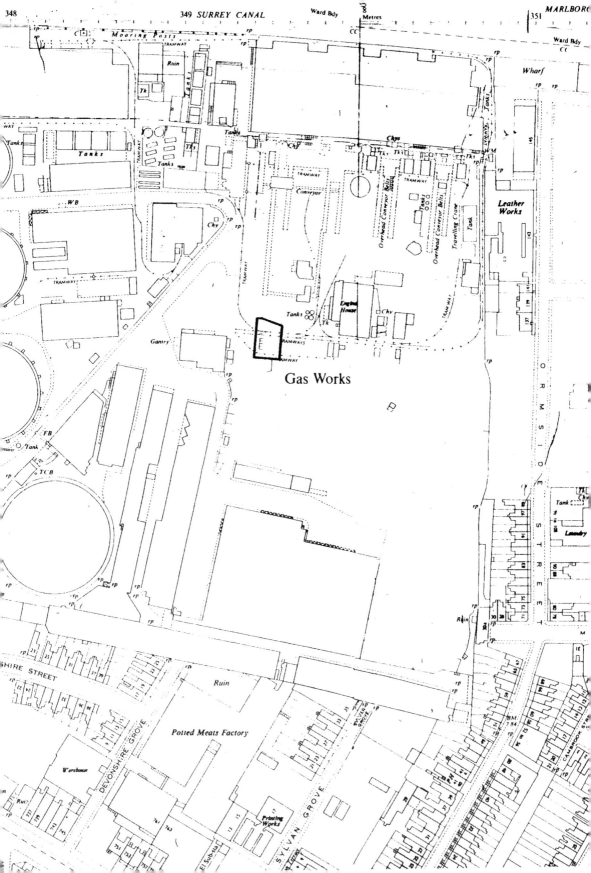

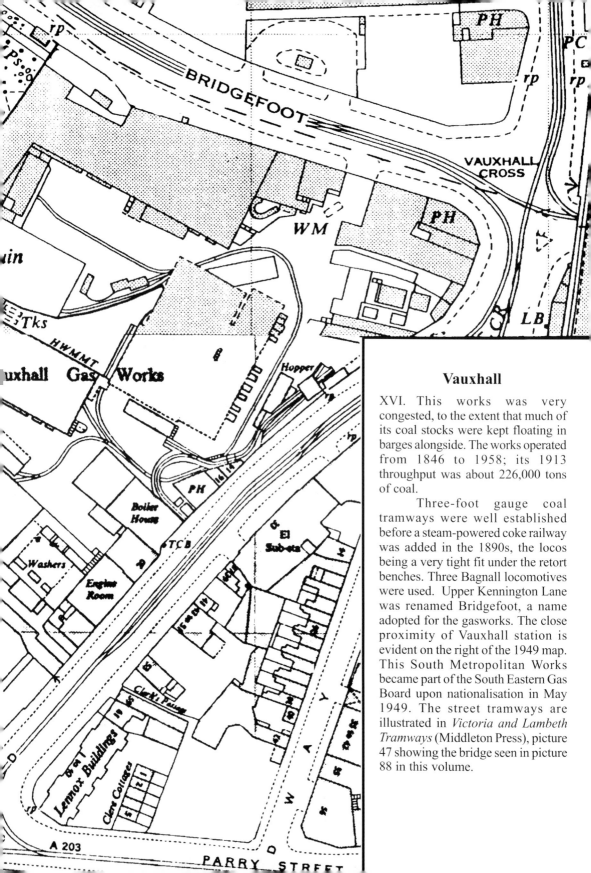

PH
PC
rp
rp

BRIDGEFOOT

rp

VAUXHALL CROSS

WM

PH

ain

Tks

HWMMT

uxhall Gas Works

Hopper

rp

PH

CR

LB

Boiler House

TCB

Washers

Engine Room

El Sub-sta

Lennox Buildings

Clare Cottages

Clark's Passage

A 203

PARRY STREET

Vauxhall

XVI. This works was very congested, to the extent that much of its coal stocks were kept floating in barges alongside. The works operated from 1846 to 1958; its 1913 throughput was about 226,000 tons of coal.

Three-foot gauge coal tramways were well established before a steam-powered coke railway was added in the 1890s, the locos being a very tight fit under the retort benches. Three Bagnall locomotives were used. Upper Kennington Lane was renamed Bridgefoot, a name adopted for the gasworks. The close proximity of Vauxhall station is evident on the right of the 1949 map. This South Metropolitan Works became part of the South Eastern Gas Board upon nationalisation in May 1949. The street tramways are illustrated in *Victoria and Lambeth Tramways* (Middleton Press), picture 47 showing the bridge seen in picture 88 in this volume.

90.   *Orion* was adorned with a headlamp, near which lies one of the massive coke shovels. The smoky, sulphurous and dusty atmosphere of such works is difficult to convey in words. (J.H.Meredith coll.)

Jason was one of the trio from W.G.Bagnall in 1898, the drawing showing its details when new. Note that there was no access from this side.

91.   *Vulcan* is seen on 13th April 1951 with its firing irons hanging on the cab backplate. The wing tank helped to balance the weight of the firebox over the short wheelbase. (J.H.Meredith)

92.   The road was constructed by Canadian contractors Stewart & McDonald in 1924-25. Hence the presence of a North American style 0-4-0ST, built by Davenport in the USA. (C.Hamilton Ellis/R.C.Riley coll.)

SEWAGE WORKS

Much of the waste water of outer South London and central North Surrey was directed to the Wandle Valley, between Croydon and Wandsworth. It was the cradle of the Industrial Revolution in the South of England and so was well endowed with scars and inelegant buildings when sewage works were required in the Mid-Victorian period. There was a railway at Merton (see IRSE no. 112) for the Wandle Valley Joint Sewerage Board. To the west, the Hogsmill Valley served part of the same area with works between New Malden and Berrylands for Surbiton Borough Council, the Borough of Malden & Coombe and the Hogsmill Valley Joint Sewerage Board.

93.   The Hogsmill Works became the property of the North Surrey Joint Sewerage Board and their new locomotive shed was photographed in April 1963. Outside it is Hunslet no. 1962 of 1939, which was shared with the New Malden Works. (C.G.Down)

94.   Hibberd no. 2201 of 1939 was recorded at Surbiton Works on 21st December 1962, when the smell was at its lowest level. Mid-Summer was a time to be avoided. (C.G.Down)

SUTTON COMMON
(SOUTHERN RAILWAY LINE CONSTRUCTION)

95.   Much of the Sutton-Wimbledon line was built using a 3ft 6ins gauge temporary line - see nos. 49 and 50 in IRSE and 46-48 in *Lines around Wimbledon* (Middleton Press). No. 12 was built by Hudswell Clarke in 1913 for the 3ft gauge lines. (J.K.Williams coll.)

96.   No. 64 was from the same manufacturer and was new to Sir Robert McAlpine & Sons in November 1925, for use on a contract on the Gold Coast. The 0-6-0T started work here soon after construction of the steeply graded route began in July 1928. (J.K.Williams coll.)

97.   No. 37 was completed by Hudswell Clarke in 1924 and was photographed in 1929. The route was designed for electric traction and was opened in two stages, the final one being on 5th January 1930. (H.F.Wheeller/R.S.Carpenter)

WATERWORKS, HAMPTON

98.   The locomotives were always immaculate and *Hampton* has its owner's name above its front buffer. The original owning water companies of the works in the background were (from left to right) West Middlesex, Grand Junction and Southwark & Vauxhall. The later pumps of the latter were east of the Lower Sunbury Road. The various Cornish beam engines used a total of about 110 tons of coal daily. (J.K.Williams coll.)

99.   *Sunbury* is pictured with some of the 140 wagons that were used on the 3½ miles of track. The bank of one of the reservoirs is on the left. A vast quantity of sand was required for the filter beds. (J.K.Williams coll.)

The Grand Junction Water Works Co. established works at Chelsea in 1820 and Kew Bridge in 1835, and supplied an area from Mayfair westwards. The Southwark & Vauxhall Water Co. was formed in 1845 and had a works at Battersea, which supplied South London as far as Nunhead. In 1852, the Metropolis Water Act prohibited the abstraction of Thames water below Teddington Lock, which resulted in these companies all building new works at Hampton. In 1902 they came under the control of the Metropolitan Water Board whose programme of improvement included the provision of a 2ft gauge railway between the works at Kempton Park and Hampton, with a branch to their coal bunkers at the wharf on the Thames. The lines were opened in 1915 and three identical 0-4-2Ts were built by Kerr, Stuart & Co. (nos. 2366-2368) to work the system. A new works, with steam turbines and coal conveyors, was opened in 1936 and railway use diminished. The rails were lifted in 1947.

100. *Sunbury* stands outside the engine shed at Hampton with some one-ton capacity tipping wagons in the background, near the West Middlesex Works. It is top centre on the left page of map XVII. Other pictures and maps are to be found in our *Kingston & Hounslow Loops*, which includes the Shepperton branch. (J.K.Williams coll.)

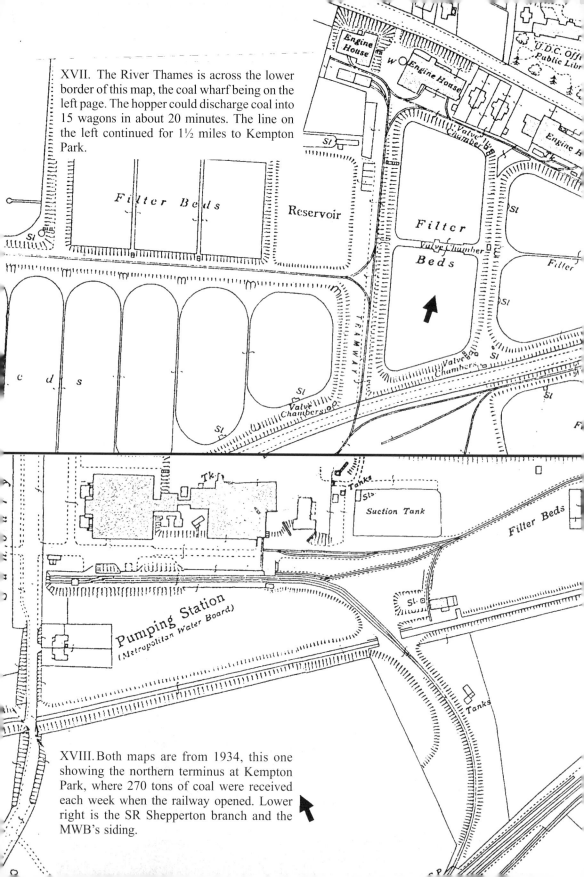

XVII. The River Thames is across the lower border of this map, the coal wharf being on the left page. The hopper could discharge coal into 15 wagons in about 20 minutes. The line on the left continued for 1½ miles to Kempton Park.

Filter Beds

Reservoir

Filter Beds

Filter

c d s

Engine House

Engine House

Engine H

Valve Chamber

Valve Chamber

Valve Chambers

Valve Chambers

U.D.C. Off
Public Libr

TRAMWAY

St

St

St

St

St

St

St

F

XVIII. Both maps are from 1934, this one showing the northern terminus at Kempton Park, where 270 tons of coal were received each week when the railway opened. Lower right is the SR Shepperton branch and the MWB's siding.

Pumping Station
(Metropolitan Water Board)

Tk

Tanks

Suction Tank

Filter Beds

Tanks

St

St

101. This fine portrait of *Sunbury* includes the chief engineer's house, which your scribe (Vic Mitchell) often visited and where he gained an appreciation of fine two-foot gauge engines. The locomotives worked hard on the 1 in 20 gradient under the bridge carrying the A308, the Upper Sunbury Road. (J.K.Williams coll.)

102.   *Kempton* stands near the gated crossing over the Lower Sunbury Road, the other being over Kempton Lane. The crew are looking towards the wharf on which the Thames Water offices now stand. (J.K.Williams coll.)

WOODSIDE BRICKWORKS, NORWOOD

103.   This 1949 diesel was provided new by Ruston & Hornsby, works no. 260744, along with no. 285297. It is at the foot of one of two inclines from the clay pit, this one being single track. The date is 30th October 1962 for this and the next picture. (C.G.Down)

104. This view, from near the works, is of the double track incline. Handleys Ltd had been succeeded by Woodside Brickworks (Croydon) Ltd. (C.G.Down)

105. A September 1967 panorama includes the double track incline and locomotive shed, after closure of the works. Five R&H diesels dating from 1934 to 1953 had earlier been in use. (C.G.Down)

5. Military
DEPTFORD SPECIAL
RESERVE DEPOT

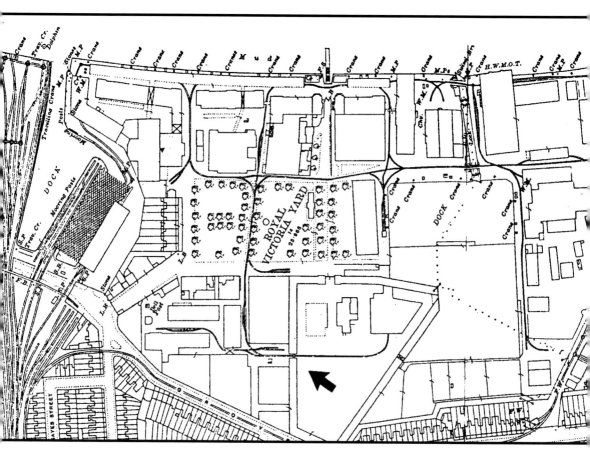

XIX.   A national food crisis developed as World War I dragged on and the Government created an emergency meat depot south of Deptford Dock (left) in 1917. It was used again during WWII. The extensive 18ins gauge system is shown on this 1916 edition at 20ins to 1 mile. The standard gauge line running along Grove Street (lower) came into use in 1900 when the City of London Corporation opened its Foreign Cattle Market. This tramway is shown in pictures 34 and 35 in our *London Bridge to East Croydon* album.

106. Four identical 0-4-0WTs were provided by the Hunslet Engine Co. Ltd in 1917. The Government also ordered a large number of ploughing engines that year, in a desperate attempt to increase home food production. (J.K.Williams coll.)

WOOLWICH ROYAL ARSENAL

107. The site covered a staggering 1300 acres and an 18ins gauge network was begun in 1873 to supplement the standard gauge sidings. *Manchester* arrived from the Avonside Engine Company as part of a batch of 16 in 1916. It lasted until about 1954. (J.K.Williams coll.)

108.   There was an extensive fleet of coaches in use, this example being first-class for the use of officers and management only. Second-class and open vehicles for workmen are shown in picture 79 in our *Charing Cross to Dartford* album. There was also a narrow gauge system in the nearby Royal Dockyard. (J.K.Williams coll.)

109.   There were 71 different narrow gauge steam locomotives listed, together with eight internal combustion engines. Of the former, 23 were supplied in 1885-86 and 25 in 1915-16. *Cormorant* was an 0-4-2T from John Fowler in 1885. Other locomotives are shown in IRSE nos. 83-87. There was also some 2ft gauge track, some triple sections being recorded at the "tumps" east of the town. (J.K.Williams coll.)

6. Pleasure

BATTERSEA PARK

"NELLIE" THE FAR TOTTERING AND OYSTERCREEK RAILWAY, FESTIVAL GARDENS, BATTERSEA PARK.

110. The Far Tottering and Oystercreek Railway opened in 1951 as an attraction at the Festival Pleasure Gardens for the Festival of Britain. The track was laid to 15ins gauge and was about ½ mile long. The stock design was by Roland Emett, then a well known cartoonist for "Punch". No. 1 *Nellie* was a standard Emett locomotive; the other two were "specials". (J.K.Williams coll.)

111.   *Nellie* waits for no. 3 *Wild Goose* to arrive at Far Tottering on 14th June 1951. The boiler is roped like a hot air balloon of the period, the cab being a replica of a balloonist's wicker basket. The tender carried the words AIR SERVICE. (J.H.Meredith)

113.   Oystercreek station and its bizarre signalling were recorded in August 1951. The line ran for a further two years. The mangle provided in place of a lever frame is evident in picture 111. (H.C.Casserley)

112.   No. 2 *Neptune* had a nautical theme with paddle wheel splashers, a divers helmet dome, a navigators wheel regulator and sundry sailing and fishing items aft thereof. Only an imprint of the lifebelt remains on its tender. (H.C.Casserley)

114.   Opening in the same park in 1954 was the Lakeside Miniature Railway. Like the three Emett locomotives, this had an ex-WWII searchlight unit (a Fordson diesel generator) in the tender with an electric motor driving the 4-6-2 locomotive. Eight machines of this type were built by Harry Barlow in Southport, but with different bodies. Six survive, but Emett's creations were destroyed in 1955 and rebodied. The termini were named Queens Road and Chelsea Bridge. (J.H.Meredith)

115.   Expo Steam in Battersea Park in 1972 used a temporary line supplied for the event by Pleasurerail and had J.B.Latham's privately owned Hunslet no. 554 *Lilla* for motive power. (P.Nicholson)

CHESSINGTON ZOO

116.   A 12ins gauge railway was laid down in 1937 and during World War II it ran on town gas - see picture 69 in our *Wimbledon to Epsom* album. It was replaced by a 2ft gauge line, seen under construction in August 1970. (P.Nicholson)

117.   Operation continued until 1978, this replica *Rocket* having a diesel engine in its tender to provide power for those needing such entertainment. (P.Nicholson)

KEW BRIDGE STEAM MUSEUM

118. Only the workshop of the mighty pumping station appears in this April 1981 view of Peckett 0-4-0ST *Triassic*. This length of temporary track is on the north side of the site. A permanent line was laid in 1986 and it extended along the western and southern boundaries as well. The Hampshire Narrow Gauge Railway Society joined forces with the Museum in 1992, bringing both stock and expertise. (P.Nicholson)

119.   *Lilla* is seen again, this time near the south wall, outside the engine shed on 28th February 1987. It has subsequently offered brief driving experiences on a siding at Porthmadog Harbour station on the Ffestiniog Railway. (J.H.Williams)

120.   A photograph from June 1999 features no. 2 *Alistair*, a Lister diesel of 1958, the passenger stock and no. 1 *Wendy*, a Bagnall from 1919. For details of steaming days of the railway and the gigantic beam engine, telephone 020 8568 4757. (P.G.Barnes)

MP Middleton Press

Easebourne Lane, Midhurst, W Sussex. GU29 9AZ Tel: 01730 813169 Fax: 01730 812601
*If books are not available from your local transport stockist, order direct with cheque,
Visa or Mastercard, post free UK.*

BRANCH LINES

Branch Line to Allhallows
Branch Line to Alton
Branch Lines around Ascot
Branch Line to Ashburton
Branch Lines around Bodmin
Branch Line to Bude
Branch Lines around Canterbury
Branch Lines around Chard & Yeovil
Branch Line to Cheddar
Branch Lines around Cromer
Branch Lines to East Grinstead
Branch Lines of East London
Branch Lines to Effingham Junction
Branch Lines around Exmouth
Branch Lines to Falmouth, Helston & St. Ives
Branch Line to Fairford
Branch Lines around Gosport
Branch Line to Hayling
Branch Lines to Henley, Windsor & Marlow
Branch Line to Hawkhurst
Branch Lines around Huntingdon
Branch Line to Ilfracombe
Branch Line to Kingsbridge
Branch Line to Kingswear
Branch Line to Lambourn
Branch Lines to Launceston & Princetown
Branch Line to Looe
Branch Line to Lyme Regis
Branch Lines around Midhurst
Branch Line to Minehead
Branch Line to Moretonhampstead
Branch Lines to Newport
Branch Lines to Newquay
Branch Lines around North Woolwich
Branch Line to Padstow
Branch Lines around Plymouth
Branch Lines to Seaton and Sidmouth
Branch Lines around Sheerness
Branch Line to Shrewsbury
Branch Line to Swanage *updated*
Branch Line to Tenterden
Branch Lines around Tiverton
Branch Lines to Torrington
Branch Line to Upwell
Branch Lines of West London
Branch Lines around Weymouth
Branch Lines around Wimborne
Branch Lines around Wisbech

NARROW GAUGE

Branch Line to Lynton
Branch Lines around Portmadoc 1923-46
Branch Lines around Porthmadog 1954-94
Branch Line to Southwold
Douglas to Port Erin
Douglas to Peel
Kent Narrow Gauge
Northern France Narrow Gauge
Romneyrail
Southern France Narrow Gauge
Sussex Narrow Gauge
Surrey Narrow Gauge
Two-Foot Gauge Survivors
Vivarais Narrow Gauge

SOUTH COAST RAILWAYS

Ashford to Dover

Bournemouth to Weymouth
Brighton to Worthing
Eastbourne to Hastings
Hastings to Ashford
Portsmouth to Southampton
Ryde to Ventnor
Southampton to Bournemouth

SOUTHERN MAIN LINES

Basingstoke to Salisbury
Bromley South to Rochester
Crawley to Littlehampton
Dartford to Sittingbourne
East Croydon to Three Bridges
Epsom to Horsham
Exeter to Barnstaple
Exeter to Tavistock
Faversham to Dover
London Bridge to East Croydon
Orpington to Tonbridge
Tonbridge to Hastings
Salisbury to Yeovil
Sittingbourne to Ramsgate
Swanley to Ashford
Tavistock to Plymouth
Three Bridges to Brighton
Victoria to Bromley South
Victoria to East Croydon
Waterloo to Windsor
Waterloo to Woking
Woking to Portsmouth
Woking to Southampton
Yeovil to Exeter

EASTERN MAIN LINES

Barking to Southend
Ely to Kings Lynn
Ely to Norwich
Fenchurch Street to Barking
Ilford to Shenfield
Ipswich to Saxmundham
Liverpool Street to Ilford
Saxmundham to Yarmouth
Tilbury Loop

WESTERN MAIN LINES

Didcot to Swindon
Ealing to Slough
Exeter to Newton Abbot
Newton Abbot to Plymouth
Newbury to Westbury
Paddington to Ealing
Paddington to Princes Risborough
Plymouth to St. Austell
Princes Risborough to Banbury
Reading to Didcot
Slough to Newbury
St. Austell to Penzance
Swindon to Bristol
Taunton to Exeter
Westbury to Taunton

MIDLAND MAIN LINES

Euston to Harrow & Wealdstone
St. Pancras to St. Albans

COUNTRY RAILWAY ROUTES

Abergavenny to Merthyr
Andover to Southampton
Bath to Evercreech Junction
Bath Green Park to Bristol
Bournemouth to Evercreech Junction
Burnham to Evercreech Junction
Cheltenham to Andover
Croydon to East Grinstead
Didcot to Winchester
East Kent Light Railway
Fareham to Salisbury
Guildford to Redhill
Reading to Basingstoke
Reading to Guildford
Redhill to Ashford
Salisbury to Westbury
Stratford upon Avon to Cheltenham
Strood to Paddock Wood
Taunton to Barnstaple
Wenford Bridge to Fowey
Westbury to Bath
Woking to Alton
Yeovil to Dorchester

GREAT RAILWAY ERAS

Ashford from Steam to Eurostar
Clapham Junction 50 years of change
Festiniog in the Fifties
Festiniog in the Sixties
Festiniog 50 years of enterprise
Isle of Wight Lines 50 years of change
Railways to Victory 1944-46
Return to Blaenau 1970-82
SECR Centenary album
Talyllyn 50 years of change
Yeovil 50 years of change

LONDON SUBURBAN RAILWAYS

Caterham and Tattenham Corner
Charing Cross to Dartford
Clapham Jn. to Beckenham Jn.
Crystal Palace (HL) & Catford Loop
East London Line
Finsbury Park to Alexandra Palace
Holborn Viaduct to Lewisham
Kingston and Hounslow Loops
Lewisham to Dartford
Lines around Wimbledon
Liverpool Street to Chingford
London Bridge to Addiscombe
Mitcham Junction Lines
North London Line
South London Line
West Croydon to Epsom
West London Line
Willesden Junction to Richmond
Wimbledon to Beckenham
Wimbledon to Epsom

STEAMING THROUGH

Steaming through Cornwall
Steaming through the Isle of Wight
Steaming through Kent
Steaming through West Hants
Steaming through West Sussex

TRAMWAY CLASSICS

Aldgate & Stepney Tramways
Barnet & Finchley Tramways
Bath Tramways
Brighton's Tramways
Bristol's Tramways
Burton & Ashby Tramways
Camberwell & W.Norwood Tramways
Clapham & Streatham Tramways
Croydon's Tramways
Dover's Tramways
East Ham & West Ham Tramways
Edgware and Willesden Tramways
Eltham & Woolwich Tramways
Embankment & Waterloo Tramways
Enfield & Wood Green Tramways
Exeter & Taunton Tramways
Greenwich & Dartford Tramways
Hammersmith & Hounslow Tramways
Hampstead & Highgate Tramways
Hastings Tramways
Holborn & Finsbury Tramways
Ilford & Barking Tramways
Kingston & Wimbledon Tramways
Lewisham & Catford Tramways
Liverpool Tramways 1. Eastern Routes
Liverpool Tramways 2. Southern Routes
Liverpool Tramways 3. Northern Routes
Maidstone & Chatham Tramways
Margate to Ramsgate
North Kent Tramways
Norwich Tramways
Reading Tramways
Seaton & Eastbourne Tramways
Shepherds Bush & Uxbridge Tramways
Southend-on-sea Tramways
Southwark & Deptford Tramways
Stamford Hill Tramways
Twickenham & Kingston Tramways
Victoria & Lambeth Tramways
Waltham Cross & Edmonton Tramways
Walthamstow & Leyton Tramways
Wandsworth & Battersea Tramways

TROLLEYBUS CLASSICS

Croydon Trolleybuses
Derby Trolleybuses
Hastings Trolleybuses
Huddersfield Trolleybuses
Maidstone Trolleybuses
Portsmouth Trolleybuses
Woolwich & Dartford Trolleybuses

WATERWAY ALBUMS

Kent and East Sussex Waterways
London to Portsmouth Waterway
West Sussex Waterways

MILITARY BOOKS

Battle over Portsmouth
Battle over Sussex 1940
Bombers over Sussex 1943-45
Bognor at War
Military Defence of West Sussex
Military Signals from the South Coast
Secret Sussex Resistance
Surrey Home Guard

OTHER RAILWAY BOOKS

Index to all Middleton Press stations
Industrial Railways of the South-East
South Eastern & Chatham Railway
London Chatham & Dover Railway
War on the Line (SR 1939-45)

BIOGRAPHY

Garraway Father & Son